Inspired to Write

WRITING WORKBOOK

30 DAYS OF PROMPTS, ACTIVITIES & ENCOURAGEMENT TO GET YOUR DREAM GOING

MILK & HONEY Books

WWW.MILKANDHONEYBOOKS.COM
SIGN UP ONLINE FOR FREE PRINTABLES AND MORE

Inspired to Write: Writing Workbook
Copyright © 2020 by Milk & Honey Books, LLC

This book is available through www.milkandhoneybooks.com and other online outlets

Created via Canva Pro
Some images and graphics from Canva & Deposit Photos

Reach us on the Internet: www.milkandhoneybooks.com
ISBN TP: 978-1-953000-04-0

This Workbook Belongs to:

Name:

Contact Info:

Journal Start Date:

If you are interested in writing
Christ-Centered, Inspirational books and
resources, check out
www.milkandhoneybooks.com for more
services, tips and opportunities.

Welcome to Your
Inspired to Write
Workbook

Hello Friend!

I'VE HAD SEVERAL PEOPLE TELL ME HOW THEY FELT LIKE THEY WERE SUPPOSED TO WRITE BUT EITHER NEEDED HELP GETTING STARTED OR NEEDED MORE INFORMATION ABOUT PUBLISHING. I NEVER IMAGINED THAT I WOULD BE ABLE TO PROVIDE VALUABLE ENCOURAGEMENT TO PEOPLE IN THIS AREA. I'VE CURRENTLY PUBLISHED TWO NON-FICTION BOOKS, ONE CO-PUBLISHED WITH A TRADITIONAL PUBLISHER AND THE OTHER INDEPENDENTLY PUBLISHED. I'VE ALSO RELEASED SEVERAL DEVOTIONALS, JOURNALS, PLANNERS, STUDY GUIDES AND WORKBOOKS LIKE THE ONE YOU HOLD IN YOUR HAND. WITH THESE EXPERIENCES I'VE GOTTEN A DEEPER INSIGHT INTO THE PROCESS, EVEN THOUGH I CONTINUE TO LEARN MORE. BUT I AM EXCITED AND PASSIONATE ABOUT BRINGING OTHERS WITH ME IN THIS JOURNEY. I'M A FIRM BELIEVER THAT IF YOU FEEL CALLED TO WRITE, THEN THE PEOPLE AROUND YOU, THE PEOPLE COMING BEHIND YOU AND YOU YOURSELF NEED THOSE WORDS. IT IS THE GIFT OF GOD IN YOU EXPRESSED THROUGH WRITING AND THERE IS NO BETTER TIME THAN NOW TO GET THAT OUT.

YOU ARE INVITED TO JOIN ME IN THIS MONTH LONG PROCESS TO HELP YOU GET STARTED OR TO HELP YOU CONTINUE IN YOUR WRITING JOURNEY. ALTHOUGH I FEEL THAT THIS BOOK CAN BENEFIT ANY WRITER, WE ARE NOT SHY ABOUT OUR FAITH AROUND HERE. THIS WORKBOOK IS GEARED TOWARDS THOSE WHO ESPECIALLY FEEL LED TO WRITE ENCOURAGING AND INSPIRATIONAL CHRIST-CENTERED BOOKS, BLOGS, CONTENT, ETC. MAYBE YOU ARE JUST ONE MONTH AWAY FROM GAINING SUBSTANTIAL PROGRESS IN YOUR WRITING JOURNEY. AND THOSE WORDS YOU RELEASE HAVE THE POTENTIAL TO SPREAD MUCH LIGHT AND HOPE.

—Jenny Erlingsson,
founder of Milk & Honey Books

Core Components

- **ESTABLISH:** We will start by getting our mind and space together, establishing some routines, and dreaming with God. What are those words that you are supposed to release and what keeps you from doing so?

- **CULTIVATE:** Next, we will work on getting out some themes and topics that relate to what's in you and what you've been through. We will also set some word count goals and start getting those words out with consistent writing.

- **PLAN:** At the end of this workbook is a 3 month and/or 15 week planner. Use this to continue your journey, keep up withe the daily routines you've set and stay accountable with your word count goals. The planner is set up in a way to keep your schedule and/or to fill the time blocks with notes, ideas and inspiration. (**IF YOU HAVE THE FREE PRINTABLE WORKBOOK, YOU CAN PURCHASE A PLANNER SEPARATELY**)

- **ACTIVITIES:** THERE ARE VARIOUS PAGES WITHIN THIS WORKBOOK THAT ALLOW YOU TO BRAINSTORM IN CREATIVE WAYS. THEY ARE NOT MEANT TO BOX YOU IN BUT RATHER HELP YOU SEE YOUR IDEAS IN A DIFFERENT WAY.

- **WORD COUNT:** THE AMOUNT OF YOUR WORDS DO MATTER. WHETHER YOU ARE WRITING FOR A BLOG OR EMAIL OR FULL MANUSCRIPT, THE NUMBER OF WORDS YOU WRITE DETERMINE THE TYPE OF BOOK, FORMAT AND EVEN GENRE. SETTING GOALS FOR THE WORDS YOU WRITE EACH DAY HELP YOU STAY CONSISTENT AND ACCOUNTABLE TO YOUR DREAM. IF YOU MISS A FEW DAYS, IT'S OK! JUST PICK IT UP AGAIN THE NEXT DAY!

- **ROUTINE:** HAVING CONSISTENT ROUTINES EQUIPS YOU WITH THE TOOLS YOU NEED TO MOVE FROM A HEALTHY, GROUNDED PLACE BUILT ON THE CORNERSTONE OF JESUS. ON THE SECOND DAY YOU WILL HAVE THE OPPORTUNITY TO WRITE DOWN WHAT THOSE ROUTINES NEED TO BE FOR YOU, ASSIGN A LETTER, NUMBER OR SYMBOL TO THEM AND THEN IMPLEMENT THEM INTO THE ROUTINE TRACKER PORTION OF THE PLANNER **IF** THAT IS INCLUDED IN YOUR WORKBOOK.

- **BE CREATIVE:** THERE ARE **RANDOM BOXES** IN THE WORKBOOK FOR WHATEVER YOU WANT TO DO WITH THEM. THEY ARE PLACES TO JOT DOWN NOTES AS INSPIRATION HITS. IN ADDITION TO THE JOURNAL & GRID PAGES, YOU CAN ALSO PRINT OFF A FREE BOOKMARK AT WWW.MILKANDHONEYWOMEN.COM.

Welcome friend! Go ahead. Breathe deep. Fill your lungs with all the assurance and permission you need. We are going to move mountains, you and I. One letter, word, sentence at a time. Take a few moments to read an excerpt from this devotion that was original published in an email series for Arise of EastWest Ministries (https://www.eastwest.org/Arise/). This ministry is special to my heart. After the director's daughter found my book on Amazon, she invited me to speak to her group in Dallas, all the way from Iceland! Even more amazing is that this ministry is geared toward missions. It was this beautiful confirmation of how God can use our voices, even in the seasons we think it is more quiet than others.

• •

"Then the Lord God formed a man from the dust of the ground and breathed into his nostrils the breath of life, and the man became a living being."
Genesis 2:7 NIV

God breathed into us. The presence of the living God, bringing life and animation to worthless clay, sparking our hearts with the imprint of the divine. He reached down to kiss us and release in us inspiration. The starting point for creativity and solution and wisdom and all that we need to breathe back out the declarations that can shape what we have dominion over.

God's breath in us gives the power to our words, running through our vocal cords, sending vibrations that release tones and timbre to our voices. That air mingling with the blood that mingles with our DNA that releases a unique sound unlike anyone else.

What beautiful creatures we are, you and I. Is it any wonder that when the Lord brought us forth he said "it is good"? And even more so, how amazing is it that we creatures of dust and clay, so imperfect and sinful and unrighteous can be made righteous and cleansed and whole through the precious blood of Jesus. We can then make impact, operating as the Lord originally intended through the empowerment and indwelling of Holy Spirit. It is this voice and this agreement with the work of Christ that allows us to triumph over every plan of the enemy.

"They triumphed over him by the blood of the Lamb and by the word of their testimony."
Revelation 12:11a

 THERE ARE BOXES LIKE THIS ALL THROUGH THIS BOOK. USE THESE FOR THE RANDOM NOTES AND INSPIRATION THAT MAY POP UP AS YOU GO THROUGH.

This is the voice that is within you. And it is made even more potent and impactful through the journey that you've been through. We overcome and see triumph take place over the enemy of our souls when Jesus' blood and those words of our stories mingle and intertwine again and again. We were not meant to be silent, we were not meant to hold back. We were meant to speak out and declare, operating as our Father does. The manner of your speaking and the sound of your voice may differ and may not sound like the person next to you. But it is meant to be released nonetheless. Even the softest whisper, overflowing from an abiding heart, can shake the foundations, can make walls crumble.

We have permission to speak because we were first spoken to, we were first sung over by the Lord. What we release is not merely random words. We are not just trying to speak to make a way for ourselves so that we can merely be heard. Our voices being released are in response to the one who loved us first. It is an act of worship that comes from the overflow of the Lord's work in our life. We release breath because he first breathed his breath into us. It is the natural outcome in this supernatural life we live as believers in Jesus. As we ourselves release our breath and raise our voices we then become the literally inspiration for others to do the same. We release the "inspiration" that others breathe in, to fill their lungs and untie their tongues to cry and call out.

"Again Jesus said, "Peace be with you! As the Father has sent me, I am sending you." And with that he breathed on them and said, "Receive the Holy Spirit.""
John 20:21&22 NIV

The Lord didn't stop at creation. He didn't stop at the Great Commission. He continues to call out, coming near, ready and willing to breathe in us and empower us with his Holy Spirit. He is the one that originated the breath in you, therefore he must remain the continual source of what we take in. If so, we must cut off every other source of toxic air. There may have been words being spoken about you and over you that were not intended to be your source not the air you breath in. It is imperative that you assess what kind of environment you are in and what air you are breathing. If what you breathe in, determines what you release, it should motivate you to find yourself in the presence of the Lord where you can breathe deeply of Him. When you operate in your creative inheritance you come into agreement with the one who the Word says "breathed out the stars". How incredibly powerful is that? This same breath that sent stars and solar systems and galaxies hurtling into space, came so low, so personally, so intimately, to breathe that same creative breath into you. So breathe deep beloved. Breathe and run.

Reflect

DAY 2

Daily Routines

Take a few moments to consider the Bible verses below:

"you also, like living stones, are being built into a spiritual house to be a holy priesthood, offering spiritual sacrifices acceptable to God through Jesus Christ. For in Scripture it says:"See, I lay a stone in Zion, a chosen and precious cornerstone,and the one who trusts in him will never be put to shame."
1 Peter 2:5&6

Cornerstones are traditionally a very important part of laying a foundation. A cornerstone is the first stone laid and then every other "stone" if you will is laid accordingly. It then orients the building in a certain direction (i). According to this verse Jesus is our cornerstone. Through Him our foundations are laid strong and secure, allowing us to be built up into people that minister to His heart and minister His heart to other people.

For those of us who desire to write words that ultimately draw people to God, we need to make sure our own foundation is anchored in Him. This doesn't have to be a huge work but is actually more effective when we take small intentional steps each day to focus on Him. For me, disciplining myself to do 5 specific things each morning as a part of my routine has been vital to my well-being. Giving me a great place to start from. In the next exercise you will have opportunity to write down what your daily foundational routine is or will be, as you prepare to write.

Here are my five:

1. Water
2. Workout
3. Word
4. Worship
5. Work

5 THINGS I DO EVERYDAY (MOSTLY)

The Gift of Reset Pt. 2

Blog post on milkandhoneywomen.com

When I do these five things, I feel refreshed, accomplished and ready to get more done. In the context of this book, this includes writing. You can read more on the blog at www.milkandhoneywomen.com and on the next page we will work on getting those routines down.

i. Architectural Cornerstones: The Meaning,History, and Intent. NewStudio Administrator
https://www.newstudioarchitecture.com/newstudio-blog/architectural-cornerstones

WHAT DOES GOD WANT TO BUILD IN YOUR LIFE THROUGH JESUS AS YOUR CORNERSTONE?

On the drawing below, write down in each block what you hear from the Lord, the passions in your heart and the goals you have.

WHAT CLUTTER DO I NEED TO CLEAR FROM MY LIFE TO BUILD FROM A CHRIST-CENTERED PLACE?

Ask the Lord to show you stumbling blocks and clutter that need to be cleared out. (Insecurity, imposter syndrome, fear of man?) Write those on the lines pointing away from the blocks. Ask the Lord to help you release those things and build what He's called you to.

Clear the Clutter

JESUS

WHAT ROUTINES DO I NEED TO SET IN PLACE TO WORK FROM A GOOD FOUNDATION?

Write down a specific routine in each line and then add a corresponding letter, number or symbol. You will use this in your planner in the back (if included) as you track routines.

9

DAY 3 — Dream with God

I find that my most authentic, core dreams are the ones god has dreamed for me first. — Jenny

Psalm 37:4 has been my favorite, foundational verse since childhood,

"Delight yourself in the Lord and he will give you the desires of you heart."

Initially I thought it was cool that God would give me everything I ever wanted. I learned quickly that this was not always the case. And honestly, I thank God for some of the prayers He didn't answer in my way. That would have been nothing but disaster.

But in these words is an invitation to know the Creator of our souls. And in doing so we become more united with His heart for us. We get a stronger sense of our place and purpose and the plans He has been setting in motion from the beginning of time. It's not just wishful thinking or thoughts tossed to the wind. In Christ we have the legitimate opportunity and ability to position ourselves in love, be anchored in hope and by faith, see Him accomplish the desires in our hearts that He put there in the first place.

Reflect

Dream with God

TAKE SOME TIME TODAY TO SEEK GOD AND ASK HIM HONESTLY. TAKE NOTE OF WHAT THOUGHTS & IMAGES RISE UP.

What brings you joy? Stirs your passion?

What have been some of your core dreams?

What have been some continual struggles?

What have you learned from your experiences?

What do you do that you know makes God smile?

Is there an overlap between all this that may be a good foundation for your book?

11

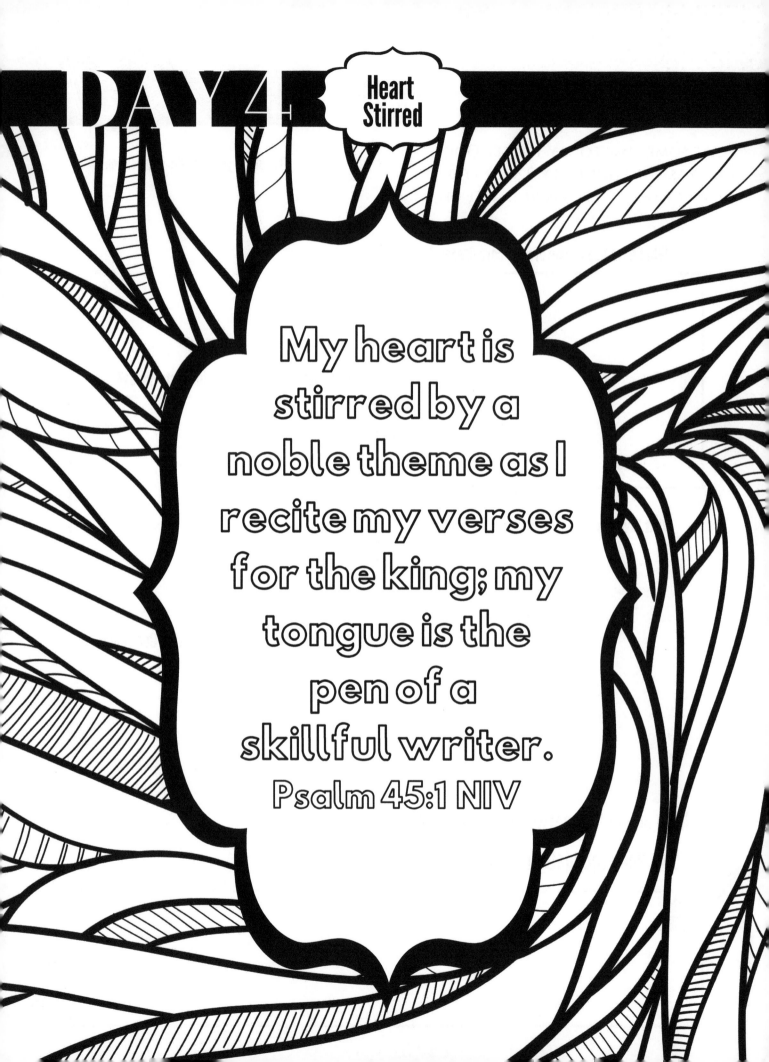

Heart Stirred

Take time today, do your routine.
Take 5 minutes or 50 and let your pen loose.
What is being stirred?
What "Noble themes" are coming to the surface?
YOU ARE BECOMING A SKILLFUL WRITER.

Reflect

Heart Stirred

Heart Stirred

DAY 5

Your theme will be the overarching message of your book. This will help in the exercise we will do tomorrow. For example, knowing the core topics and theme for my book, Milk & Honey in the Land of Fire & Ice helped me plot out my subtitle "Cultivating Sweet Spots of Christ-Centered Identity, Intimacy and Influence." The theme combines both the significant message of your book and significant takeaway for the reader.

What does this mean?

When I taught Jr. High, I made sure I had nuggets and triggers as I planned my messages. I wanted to make sure I taught the students in a way that gave them something they could carry (nuggets) and words or images that would remind them of what God spoke to them (triggers). In our current climate, "trigger" has such a negative connotation, but in this context we are looking for triggers that point back to God.

So, considering the overlap that you wrote down from the day 3 "Dreaming with God" exercise, are there some themes and/or topics that arise?

Push yourself to write out at least 20. Stretch those brainstorming muscles!

Reflect

Triggers

Nuggets

Write out at least 20 topics and/or themes. Don't worry, we will sort it all out later. Those of you who have the Milk & Honey study guide or Dwell Bible Study Journal may recognize this tree. For the purpose of this group we will be focusing on topics/themes and not verses, but you can see the intent is the same. Being rooted in Christ and letting our words overflow from that.

Influence

Intimacy

Identity

Rooted in Christ

Themes Arise

Just for fun (well, and for real), come up with 3 title ideas and 5 subtitle ideas that define your project. Research some of the books you have on your shelf. Look on Barnes and Noble or Amazon for inspiration and research. What themes and topics and words sum up your message the best?

Here are some examples with an arrow to subtitles:

JENNY ERLINGSSON

Becoming **HIS**

»»

FINDING YOUR PLACE AS A *Daughter of God*

DESTINY-DEFINI

Dwell **Bible Study & Prayer** JOURNAL

A GUIDED JOURNAL FOR STUDY, SCRIPTURE MEDITATION & PRAYER

YOU ARE A LOVED, COVERED & CREATIVE SON OF GOD!

The Daddy's BOY DEVOTIONAL

A PRAYER, PLANNING & ACTIVITY JOURNAL FOR BOYS

JENNY ERLINGSSON WITH THOR ERLINGSSON

CULTIVATING SWEET SPOTS OF CHRIST CENTERED IDENTITY, INTIMACY, & INFLUENCE IN EVERY SEASON

Milk & Honey IN THE LAND OF FIRE & ICE

JENNY ERLINGSSON FORWARD BY CHRISTA SMITH

Title Ideas

1.

2.

3.

Subtitle Ideas

1

2

3

4

5

REST, BEFORE WE REALLY DIG IN. HERE ARE SOME BRAIN-STRETCHING ACTIVITIES:

FIND THE WORDS

```
T  Y  P  I  S  T  A  R  T  I  S  T
R  U  N  E  D  I  T  O  R  K  C  R
A  V  R  U  I  K  B  P  Z  D  H  A
N  T  W  N  R  E  A  O  C  R  E  I
S  E  E  E  E  S  K  E  A  I  M  N
L  A  L  M  C  R  E  T  R  V  I  E
A  C  D  C  T  I  R  E  P  E  S  R
T  H  E  H  O  N  N  W  E  R  T  J
O  E  R  E  R  A  T  A  N  N  B
R  R  U  F  E  H  U  I  T  A  C  U
S  P  I  L  O  T  T  T  E  N  O  Y
D  O  C  X  V  V  O  E  R  N  O  E
F  L  A  W  Y  E  R  R  M  Y  K  R
```

ARTIST	DIRECTOR	TRAINER
BAKER	DRIVER	TRANSLATOR
BUYER	EDITOR	TURNER
CARPENTER	LAWYER	TUTOR
CHEF	NANNY	TYPIST
CHEMIST	NURSE	WAITER
CLEANER	PILOT	WELDER
CLERK	POET	
COOK	TEACHER	

B

A

B

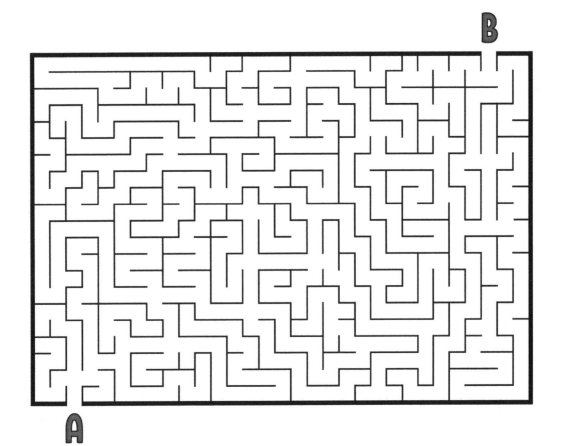

A

23

DAY 8

Is your project going to be fiction or nonfiction? Memoir, poetry, novel, devotional etc? Knowing your message, topics and themes can help you determine what kind of book you are writing.

General Definitions:

Nonfiction is a work that contains factual information. These may include self-help, how-to, memoir, biography, travel and reference books. Many of the titles written in the Christian market like Bible Studies, devotionals, and curriculum are also considered non-fiction.

Fiction books are stories that the author made up. They may have elements of truth in them or be based on a true story but they are mostly fabricated or embellished for the story.

For more information about these type of books and the specific genres under each, check out: https://reference.yourdictionary.com/books-literature/different-types-of-books.html

As you read about the different genres of books, where do you see your book fitting? It may seem like our choices are limited to Religion or Prayer or maybe even memoir but there may be other genres that fit that will help in the future as you market your book.

Reflect

 **Circle what types of book or writing appeals to you:**

instructional

Prayer

COOKBOOK

poetry book

guide

children's book

WORKBOOK

manual

ya fiction

DEVOTIONAL

memoir

ACADEMIC

memoir

adult fiction

Coloring

How-To

blog

DEVOTIONAL PLANNER

devotional journal

DAY 9

Lets plant a tree of chapter ideas, based on our Christ Centered approach. Those themes we brainstormed, what do you see as main chapters/topics? Take your list of at least 20 and slim it down to 12. You may see some topics that fit better together than standing alone. This doesn't mean your book will only have 12 chapters, sections, or topics. It just gives you a good place to start from as you think about the flow of your book. This is also good practice for working out your theme. There may be more words triggered that feed future content. Also, if you are writing a blog, not book, consider these as 12 post ideas.

Write out 12 tentative chapter titles. Then number them 1-12 based on possible flow. There are also two more sets of boxes if you want to change your order.

☐ _____ ☐ ☐

☐ _____ ☐ ☐

☐ _____ ☐ ☐

☐ _____ ☐ ☐

☐ _____ ☐ ☐

☐ _____ ☐ ☐

☐ _____ ☐ ☐

☐ _____ ☐ ☐

☐ _____ ☐ ☐

☐ _____ ☐ ☐

☐ _____ ☐ ☐

☐ _____ ☐ ☐

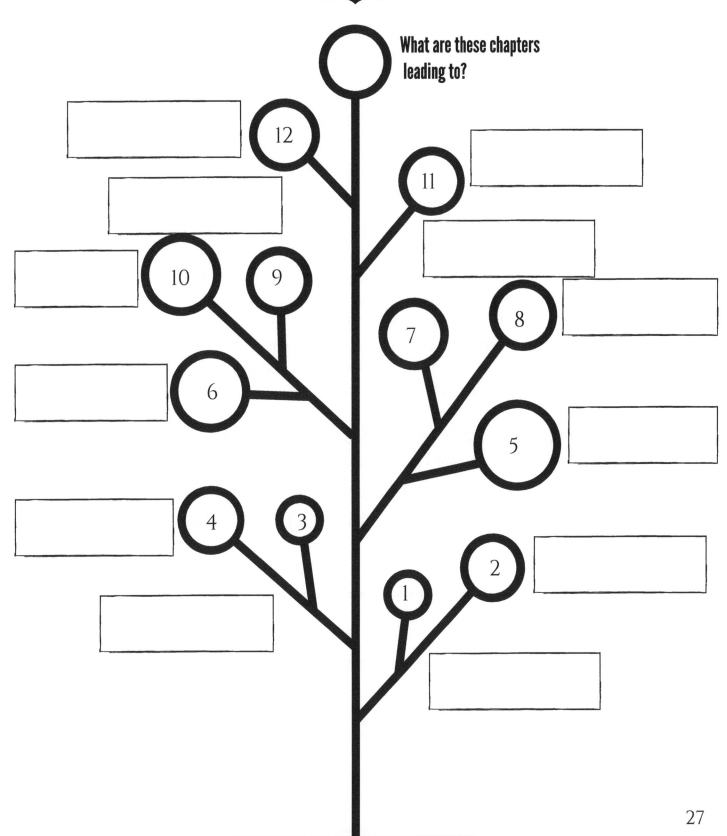

What are these chapters leading to?

12

11

10

9

8

7

6

5

4

3

2

1

I'm sure that if you have felt the call and stirring to write, there are many journals, scraps of paper, notebooks and more filled with your words. Both of my published books were initially bulked up by messages and words I had already written. This was a beautiful process as I plugged things in. Not only did it give me a lot of content to include and expound on, but it showed me how God had already been weaving the messages of my books throughout my life. There is something that God is speaking through you out of the overflow of your walk with Him and what you've been through. Going back over those things will remind you that He has indeed called you to write.

We are going to use the next few days to go through journals, notes, old unpublished writing or posts. If you have published posts with other websites, and it is relevant to your current work, double check with the host to make sure you can include that article. If you can't, it's ok, just rewrite your content in a way that fresh and unique. If you have your own blog, by all means, dig through there and pull out what fits into your current project theme. Don't forget to look at meaningful verses underlined in your Bible, random notes on your phone and even social media posts. This will be a sort of treasure hunt, allowing you to dig for jewels that are more valuable than you know.

On the next few pages, your chapter tree is broken down into 12 sections. Once again, don't let the "12" box you in. This is just a good number to work with and will most likely change based on what kind of project you are working on. Label each section with your tentative chapter headings and then fill in each section with the location, date and key notes from what you find.

Example:

CH. 3 *Making every effort*

- 2nd Peter 1:10-11
- North Carolina church message notes on phone
- blog post from September
- Notes I scribbled in blue journal. folded edge. blue ink

Your turn:

Plug It In

Plug It In

Plug It In

Plug It In

Now that you have plugged into your chapter/topic/sections, ask the Lord to give you fresh revelation. How can you expand on what you have filled in that relates to your topic and the words that have previously released?

"Write the vision; make it plain on tablets, so he may run who reads it."

Habakkuk 2:2a ESV

Reflect

DAY 14 — REST & REFLECT

Below is an excerpt from a devotional I wrote for Arise of EastWest Ministries.
You can read the full post at milkandhoneywomen.com/rhythms-of-rest-reflection.

"The Lord your God is with you, the Mighty Warrior who saves. He will take great delight in you; in His love he will no longer rebuke you, but will rejoice over you with singing." -Zephaniah 3:17

Can you hear it?
Can you pause long enough to hear the sound of His voice,
the song that He is singing over you?
I believe that this soundtrack is continuous,
whether we tap into it intentionally or not.
It's the sound of rejoicing that beckons us from the place of striving
to realizing that we are dearly loved and delighted over.
It's affirmation that we all crave,
approval that we all need.
It's found in the Lord and in that place we can truly breathe.
Taking in deep breaths of wind of His Spirit.
Releasing the stress and agreeing with the relief that His presence brings.
Through Jesus' work on the cross we have access
to more than we could have ever imagined.
He is with us.
He saves.
He takes delight in us.
He loves us.
He will no longer rebuke us.
He sings songs of pure joy over us.

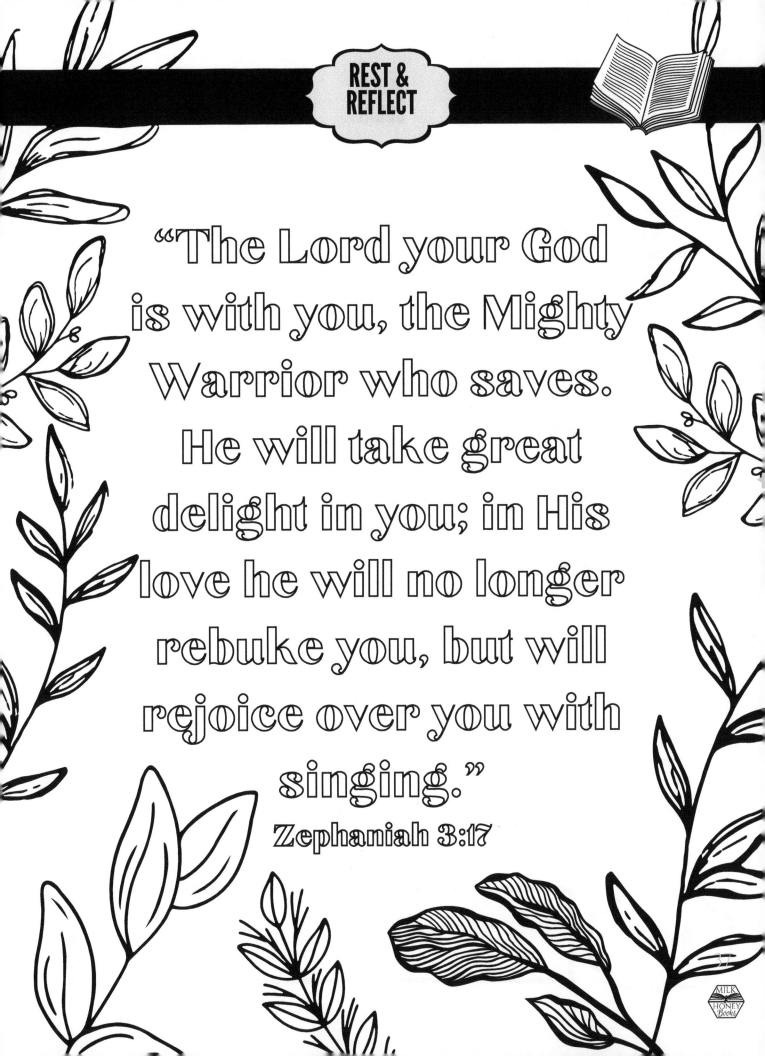

REST & REFLECT

"The Lord your God is with you, the Mighty Warrior who saves. He will take great delight in you; in His love he will no longer rebuke you, but will rejoice over you with singing."

Zephaniah 3:17

DAY 15 { Word Count }

We are going to focus on word count today. If you are a part of the Nanowrimo writing push, you know that keep up with your daily word count is a big part of the program. As you listen to other author's share you will also hear them mention word count alot.

Why is this important?

It gives you a specific, consistent goal when it comes to writing, especially a large project. If you think about having to write 30,000 to 80,000 words, that can get pretty overwhelming. But, if you focus on a specific count a day, you will conquer that mountain a bit at a time, until its done.

What can you realistically do? And also, how can you challenge yourself? Maybe your realistic word count is 500 words a day, and your challenge is...to actually write 500 words a day.

500 words is over half of an average blog post.
Done consistently for 90 days, that gives you 45,000 words.
In 3 months you could have your first draft of an average non-fiction book or short novel done.

Now how would that feel? Imagine if you were even able to write 1000 words per day, or even just 250 words a day? That discipline will give you significant progress.

Keep in mind that your job right now is <u>not to edit</u> as you go or try to write 500 perfect words per day. Your current job is to get moving, to get the words out. The editing of the 2nd and 3rd and even 4th draft of your manuscript is where the book really begins to form and shine.

{ Reflect }

Current Word
Count Goal

Remember, this is to give you a goal to shoot for. If you miss a day or two or three (because #LIFE, just pick back up again and keep moving!)

If I write [ ] words per day

for [ ] days, I will have a

[ ] word first draft!

(DIVIDE THAT BY 1000 FOR A ROUGH AMOUNT OF POTENTIAL BLOG POSTS!)

DAY 16

Write

Now that we have themes and topics and plugged in content and revelation and word count, whew, it's time to buckle down and write if you haven't already been doing so. Flex those muscles we have been stretching and put pen to paper (or fingers to keys). The next few pages will have room for you to write paragraphs or notes but I suggest taking time to transfer your outline (tree) and notes to your computer, forming the text that you will transform into your manuscript. Most people will start on Word or Pages or another type of processor. There is also another program called Scrivener that many writers use, that I love to write with as well.

Use what you have for now as you get started. Look at you! You are getting this thing going!

DAY 17

Write

Write

DAY 18
Imagine Your Cover

Have you thought about your cover yet? This may seem like thinking too far out but it is going to eventually be a part of the process if you move further with your project. Even a book that is only released in eBook form needs a front cover to display digitally.

In addition to your word count today, take some time to imagine what you want your book cover to look like. This will most definitely change and if you decide to pursue traditional publishing in the future, the publisher will have the final say. But until then, thinking about this part of your book is an important exercise in getting a feel for what you are releasing. Plus, its fun!

Look at other books, your favorite blogs, magazines and even pinterest. What inspires you? What color schemes do you like the best? What images or photos evoke the feeling and theme of your book? I suggest starting a private pinterest album full of all the things that inspire your project. It's also a good place to hold future research if applicable from different websites.

Below is a sample of Milk & Honey's full large print cover that I uploaded to Amazon & Ingram Spark to publish my book. The actual size of the final cover depends on the size of your book and number of pages. On the next page there are two front cover and one full book cover sections for you to draw, color or make notes in based on your ideas.

Imagine Your Cover

COVER 1

COVER 2

FULL COVER

DAY 19

For this reason I remind you to fan into flame the gift of God, which is in you through the laying on of my hands. For the Spirit God gave us does not make us timid, but gives us power, love and self-discipline.
2 Timothy 1:6-7 NIV

DAY 20

Write

Let us not become weary in doing good, for at the proper time we will reap a harvest if we do not give up.
Galatians 6:9 NIV

DAY 21

With our focus on word count and writing consistently, you may be feeling a little drained creatively. Remember, we are still stretching our muscles in this area so don't be disappointed if you've hit a block. Take advantage of this rest day and do something that fills you back up with creative juices.

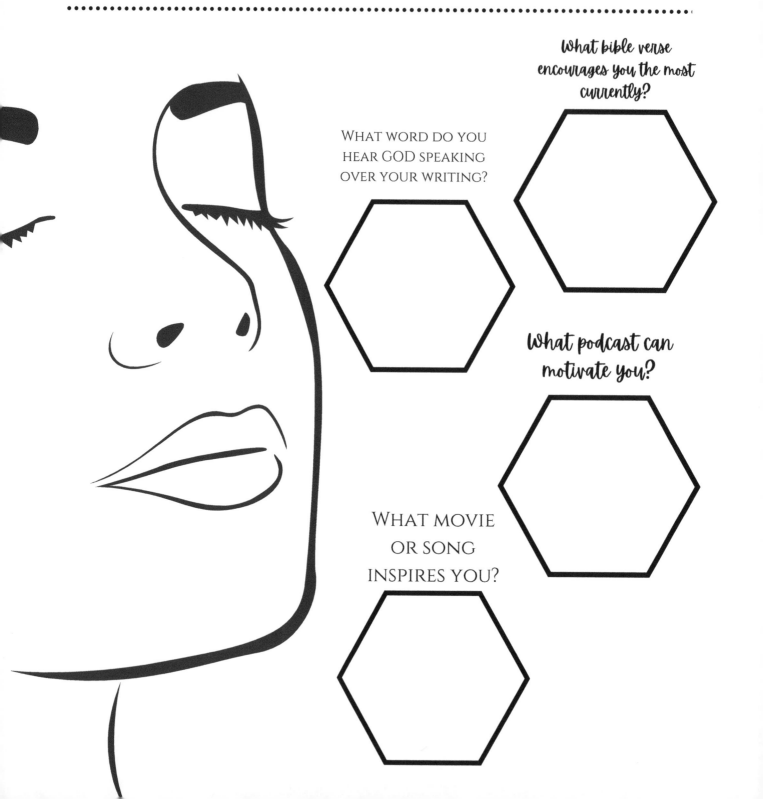

What bible verse encourages you the most currently?

WHAT WORD DO YOU HEAR GOD SPEAKING OVER YOUR WRITING?

What podcast can motivate you?

WHAT MOVIE OR SONG INSPIRES YOU?

Lord, Pour into me what needs to be poured out.

DAY 22

How was last week for you? Did you hit your writing goals in relation to word count? Re-adjust a new goal for this week. Maybe you need to stick with the same amount or less words per day. Or if you hit a good flow, maybe you can increase your daily word count. What incentive can you reward yourself with at the end of this week for meeting your goals?

This week my goal is:

If I make my goal, I will reward myself with:

If I don't make my goal, I will remember that:

What, if anything, should I change about my routine?

Is there anything I can lay down to increase my capacity for writing?

What do I want this to look like in 3 months? In 6 months?

DAY 23

Think on your relationship with Jesus today. Who does He say you are and how is that reflected in your words?

Look through old activities in this workbook and the flow of your writing. Do you see anything special, unique, or eye-opening that you haven't noticed before?

What is He whispering over you as you write?

Journal

TAKE TIME TO SIT, REST, BREATHE...BE BEFORE THE LORD.
WHAT DOES HE HAVE TO SAY TO YOU?

Reflect on Jesus

DAY 24 — Write

I have put my words in your mouth and
covered you with the shadow of my hand—
Isaiah 51:16a

Many times, we limit acts of beauty and worship to things that we deem to be in the creative artistic realm. But that is not how our God works. All of us were endowed with gifts and callings and the core purpose of all of them is to minister to our Lord and bring glory to Him.

He is looking for those who will love Him purely, giving back in joy and laughter all their favorite things. He is actively seeking according to John 4, ones who will worship Him in spirit and in truth. If He is seeking this type of authentic unboxed worship, then when you live and breathe and work in this way you are drawing His presence into whatever room you step into. You are breaking barriers by breaking open your alabaster box over and over, whatever that looks like.

I hesitate to even give you more examples because I don't want even my own limited illustrations to box you in. You know what makes your heart beat. You know what you have been holding so dear to your heart, wondering if you can trust it out there in the cold dark world. You can remember the things you enjoyed as a child before rules and responsibilities shooed them away. You know what it is that you do that causes you to sense heaven open and the smile of the Lord all over you.

For me is writing. It means the most to me, words unlock so much. And sometimes I avoid it. It's too deep, too personal, sometimes painful to see my inner musings out there on display. But when I write, and I stay and dig in, I feel like my spirit has plugged into a power source. The Holy Spirit surges in me like a stream and words and images and prose and poetry and the prophetic flow out. And the ceiling above me gets thinner and thinner and I feel God peeking over. Smiling at the scribbles of His little girl.

I'm not saying all my words make sense or are even good but when every part of me aligns with this **fingerprint of worship** that He gave me, my soul cries out. I'm there, at His feet, pouring it out, knowing that the atmosphere of my family and future and friends are shifting bit by bit because of the fragrance that fills the room.

• •

EXCERPT FROM CH. 10 OF MILK & HONEY IN THE LAND OF FIRE & ICE

WHEN YOU GET A CHANCE, REFLECT A BIT ON JOHN CHAPTER 4 AND JOHN CHAPTER 12 IN THE BIBLE

WHAT IS THIS TO YOU? WATER FROM THE WELL THAT WON'T RUN DRY OR OIL POURED OUT OVER THE FEET OF JESUS?

59

Write

DAY 27 — Target Audience

The beauty about releasing words in their various shapes and forms is that someone else can get a glimpse of something tangible that they can run with. All of this coming out of the overflow of your thoughts, ideas, stories and passions. Determining your target audience helps you figure out who is doing the running, or rather, who needs to be empwered to run. Like with many illustrations and activities in this book, the intention is not to feel like you are being locked in a box. Instead it encourages you to focus on the unique message that God has given you, finetuning it to be heard well by the ones that it is intended for.

For example, I am in community with an amazing ministry called Velvet Ashes (www.velvetashes.com). I believe that any person can find strength and encouragement through the resources that they offer. However, their target audience is women who are serving cross culturally across the world. That means their message is finely tuned to women who are dealing with culture shock, homesickness, transition to and fro, having families overseas, Third-culture kids, language issues, etc. As a woman who is serving cross-culturally in Iceland, I trust what they offer for me because I know I'm in their target. I am confident that when I read a blog post or listen to an online talk or join a connect group that they facilitate, I'm going to be able to glean what I need for where I am at.

So, who is your target audience and what do they need for where *they* are at?

Who do you think your project is for? Name 3 groups of people:

Where are they? Physically, geographically, online?

What do they need the most? What questions are they asking?

How will your words answer their questions and empower them to run?

I Write

I write because at a certain point I tire of just telling how to do something.
Letting my words be constrained and contained within a box of information
to sit on a shelf unattended and forgotten.
Never released into the atmosphere of your life and into the sky
where kingdom can rain down.

I tire of telling something that I am not willing to finish,
not willing to plant and then dig up,
let the roots down deep,
letting the fruit soar out and high.
Letting you and I taste and see that the Lord is so good and so sweet and so needed.

I write so that I can show, not just tell.
Write stories that capture you and pull you in to testimony.
Let you breathe it in,
taste of it,
be saturated in the experience of what God is doing and can do.
Calling things that are not as though they are,
writing the stories that I want to see.
 Painting a masterpiece that invites you into the story that is meant for you to color
with the image of beauty He has placed on you.

I want to write prophetically,
prose that proposes and ponders on mysteries
only available to those who will access the riches of eternity.
That declares what is not into what can be,
speaking forth with a breath of creative power what in fact should be,
on earth, as in heaven.

In this dirt bring in heaven.

So. I write. So that it shall be.

EXCERPT FROM MILK & HONEY IN THE LAND OF FIRE & ICE

What will you do today to celebrate how far you've come?

DAY 29

What's next? Take inventory of where you are at. Here is a quick quiz to find out what direction you need to go as your close out this month. Your answers will determine the best next steps for you. Things definitely change so don't feel like this defines where you are forever and always. Answer for the current season you are in.

Do you feel empowered to write and continue to do so?

A. DEFINITELY YES!!

B. A LITTLE MORE THAN BEFORE

C. NOT REALLY, FEELING OVERWELMED

How many words did you complete this month? Including the words you filled in from your other sources.

A. 10,000 AND UP

B. 5,000-10,000

C. LESS THAN 5,000

Do you feel the release to take it up a notch?

A. YES, I FEEL LIKE I AM SUPPOSED TO PUBLISH & AM EAGER TO FINISH

B. ALMOST, I'M STILL FIGURING OUT MY THEMES & MESSAGE

C. THIS WAS FUN, BUT I'M GOING TO PUT IT ON PAUSE FOR NOW

Are you interested in going the traditional publishing route or independently publishing?

A. I AM LEANING TOWARD TRADITIONAL PUBLISHING BUT WANT TO LEARN/TRY BOTH

B. I AM LEARNING TOWARD SELF-PUBLISHING BUT WANT TO LEARN/TRY BOTH WHEN I'M READY

C. I'M NOT INTERESTED IN EITHER YET

Who do you feel like your project is for? This is a combination of target audience and intended reach.

A. FOR THOSE IN MY TARGET AUDIENCE, AS FAR AS THAT REACH MAY GO.

B. FOR FAMILY/SPHERE OF INFLUENCE THAT MAY TRICKLE INTO A LARGER AUDIENCE.

C. MORE OF A PERSONAL PROJECT THAT MAY OR MAY NOT BE SHARED.

Quiz Answers

Keep in mind that these answers are not a professional opinion or even amateur opinion. They are just some ideas for you based on what you answered on the previous page. Read below, think about it, pray over it and do what you feel like God is leading you to!

Mostly A:

Now it's time to really focus and do the work needed to move your project forward. This means that you need to continue to write your book but also learn a bit more about the self-publishing process and/or prepare a proposal for an agent or editor. If you know for sure that you will publish this or another project eventually, you also need to start considering website, email list and initial forms of marketing. But don't worry, you already have what it take to get it done!

Mostly B:

You are on your way there! Keep up the good work and continue in the progress that you are making. You may feel like you are not ready to release your words but that doesn't mean you have to give up now. Continue working on your themes and topics, keeping up with word count and engaging in community. Every little thing that you do in building yourself up and putting words out will add up to significant progress and a rewarding outcome.

Mostly C:

Look at you! You did something out of your comfort and have some fruit to show for it. Even if you don't feel like the next few months is right to release a project, or even if you don't want to release one at all, I hope that you feel inspired to write words of life that will affect those around you. If you plan to keep writing, continue to look over this handbook, glean information and be faithful to the gift God has given you.

A mix of all 3:

If you got a good mix of all three then maybe you need to talk to someone to help you figure it all out! Tomorrow we will talk about more opportunities and resources that may assist you in your decision making.

I want to thank you so much for taking the time to work through this process. Whatever the outcome was for you, I know that there will be significant fruit that develops from the seeds you planted during this time. Nothing that the Lord speaks to us or through us is wasted.

I hope that yesterday's quiz gave you initial insight into what your next steps may be. For those of you that answered mostly in the A or B categories, I would like to invite you to be a part of the Influence Writer's Group on Facebook. This group is geared toward those who want to move forward with publishing and want to continue to develop their writing in a safe, celebratory place.

Milk and Honey books is not just for those who are interested in independently publishing or need help moving toward the traditional publishing route. It will continue to add services for writers and resources for those needing a little encouragement in their lives. More details can be found at www.milkandhoneybooks.com.

MILK & HONEY WRITERS
Influence Group
ENCOURAGEMENT & ACCOUNTABILITY
TO RELEASE CHRIST-CENTERED
RESOURCES

MISSION

To Cultivate Christ-Centered Identity, Intimacy and Influence by releasing books of Presence, Purpose and Promise.

VISION

Milk & Honey Books provides resources and services for those who especially want to flourish in the area of lasting influence. I believe we can do this by releasing our unique voices, in the form of the written word, to influence the unique communities we touch. It is our goal to release Non-fiction and eventually Fiction books that are encouraging, uplifting, challenging, creative, redemptive, fun, and faith based. Since we are also serving in Iceland, these services will also help provide support for our desire to see more resources translated into Icelandic.

Planning Well

On the next few pages are a 3 month planner to help you track your word count, habit, take notes and make space for your writing. There are also other resources that you may be interested in using that can be ordered off of our website. I hope these will also give you good examples of things that can be created, especially if you want to start off with a devotional or journal.

Other Books & Journals

BOOKS

Milk & Honey in the Land of Fire & Ice
Becoming His:
Finding your place as a daughter of God
Daddy's girl devotional
Daddy's boy devotional

JOURNALS & PLANNERS

Milk & Honey Women Study & Prayer Journal
Dwell Bible Study & Prayer Journal
The Cultivational Planner:
A Devotional planner for women
Faith over fear simple weekly planner & journal
Faith over fear devotional journal

Inspired to Write
3 MONTH PLANNER

Schedule
Notes
Word Count
Routine
Words

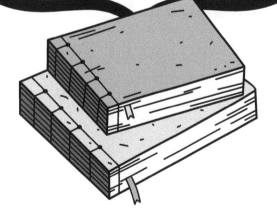

MILK & HONEY Books

Month of:

Monday

□ **morning**

Important This Week

- ⬡
- ⬡
- ⬡
- ⬡
- ⬡
- ⬡
- ⬡
- ⬡

Routine Tracker

□ □ □ □ □

afternoon

WORD COUNT GOAL

evening

Tuesday	Wednesday
morning	morning
Routine Tracker	Routine Tracker
afternoon	afternoon
evening	evening

Thursday

morning

Friday

morning

Routine Tracker

Routine Tracker

afternoon

afternoon

evening

evening

morning

morning

Routine Tracker

Routine Tracker

afternoon

afternoon

What does rest look like for you today?

evening

evening

Word Count Done

MILK HONEY Books

Month of:

Monday

morning

Important This Week

- ⬡
- ⬡
- ⬡
- ⬡
- ⬡
- ⬡
- ⬡
- ⬡

WORD COUNT GOAL

Routine Tracker

afternoon

evening

Tuesday	Wednesday
morning	morning
Routine Tracker	Routine Tracker
afternoon	afternoon
evening	evening

Thursday

Friday

morning

morning

Routine Tracker

☐ ☐ ☐ ☐ ☐

Routine Tracker

☐ ☐ ☐ ☐ ☐

afternoon

afternoon

evening

evening

Saturday

morning

Routine Tracker

afternoon

What does rest look like for you today?

evening

Sunday

morning

Routine Tracker

afternoon

evening

Word Count Done

MILK HONEY Books

morning

Important This Week

- ◯
- ◯
- ◯
- ◯
- ◯
- ◯
- ◯
- ◯

Routine Tracker

WORD COUNT GOAL

afternoon

evening

Tuesday

Wednesday

□ **morning**

□ **morning**

Routine Tracker
□ □ □ □ □

Routine Tracker
□ □ □ □ □

afternoon

afternoon

evening

evening

Thursday

morning

Routine Tracker

☐ ☐ ☐ ☐ ☐

afternoon

evening

Friday

morning

Routine Tracker

☐ ☐ ☐ ☐ ☐

afternoon

evening

Saturday

Sunday

morning

morning

Routine Tracker

Routine Tracker

afternoon

afternoon

What does rest look like for you today?

evening

evening

Word Count Done

Month of:

Monday

morning

Important This Week

Routine Tracker

afternoon

WORD COUNT GOAL

evening

morning

morning

Routine Tracker

Routine Tracker

afternoon

afternoon

evening

evening

Thursday

morning

Friday

morning

Routine Tracker

☐ ☐ ☐ ☐ ☐

Routine Tracker

☐ ☐ ☐ ☐ ☐

afternoon

afternoon

evening

evening

Saturday

Sunday

morning

morning

Routine Tracker

Routine Tracker

afternoon

afternoon

What does rest look like for you today?

evening

evening

Word Count Done

MILK HONEY Books

Month of:

Monday

Important This Week

morning

Routine Tracker

afternoon

evening

WORD
COUNT
GOAL

Tuesday

morning

Routine Tracker

afternoon

evening

Wednesday

morning

Routine Tracker

afternoon

evening

Thursday

Friday

morning

morning

Routine Tracker

☐ ☐ ☐ ☐ ☐

Routine Tracker

☐ ☐ ☐ ☐ ☐

afternoon

afternoon

evening

evening

morning

morning

Routine Tracker

Routine Tracker

afternoon

afternoon

What does rest look like for you today?

evening

evening

Word Count Done

MILK HONEY Books

Month of:

morning

Important This Week

- ⬡
- ⬡
- ⬡
- ⬡
- ⬡
- ⬡
- ⬡
- ⬡

Routine Tracker

afternoon

WORD COUNT GOAL

evening

Tuesday

Wednesday

morning

morning

Routine Tracker

Routine Tracker

afternoon

afternoon

evening

evening

Thursday

morning

Friday

morning

Routine Tracker

Routine Tracker

afternoon

afternoon

evening

evening

Saturday

morning

Routine Tracker

afternoon

What does rest look like for you today?

evening

Sunday

morning

Routine Tracker

afternoon

evening

Word Count Done

Month of:

Monday

☐ **morning**

Routine Tracker
☐ ☐ ☐ ☐ ☐

Important This Week

⬡
⬡
⬡
⬡
⬡
⬡
⬡
⬡

WORD COUNT GOAL

afternoon

evening

morning

morning

Routine Tracker

Routine Tracker

afternoon

afternoon

evening

evening

MILK HONEY Books

Thursday

Friday

morning

morning

Routine Tracker

☐ ☐ ☐ ☐ ☐

Routine Tracker

☐ ☐ ☐ ☐ ☐

afternoon

afternoon

evening

evening

morning

morning

Routine Tracker

Routine Tracker

afternoon

afternoon

What does rest look like for you today?

evening

evening

Word Count Done

MILK & HONEY Books

Month of:

Monday

Important This Week

WORD
COUNT
GOAL

morning

Routine Tracker

afternoon

evening

morning

morning

Routine Tracker

Routine Tracker

afternoon

afternoon

evening

evening

MILK
HONEY
Books

Thursday

Friday

morning

morning

Routine Tracker

Routine Tracker

afternoon

afternoon

evening

evening

Saturday

morning

Routine Tracker

afternoon

What does rest look like for you today?

evening

Sunday

morning

Routine Tracker

afternoon

evening

Word Count Done

Month of:

Monday

Important This Week

- ◯
- ◯
- ◯
- ◯
- ◯
- ◯
- ◯
- ◯

WORD COUNT GOAL

morning

Routine Tracker

afternoon

evening

morning

morning

Routine Tracker

Routine Tracker

afternoon

afternoon

evening

evening

MILK
HONEY
Books

Thursday

Friday

morning

morning

Routine Tracker

☐ ☐ ☐ ☐ ☐

Routine Tracker

☐ ☐ ☐ ☐ ☐

afternoon

afternoon

evening

evening

Saturday

morning

Routine Tracker

afternoon

What does rest look like for you today?

evening

Sunday

morning

Routine Tracker

afternoon

evening

Word Count Done

Month of:

Important This Week

- ⬡
- ⬡
- ⬡
- ⬡
- ⬡
- ⬡
- ⬡
- ⬡

WORD COUNT GOAL

_____

Monday

morning

Routine Tracker

afternoon

evening

Tuesday

morning

Routine Tracker

afternoon

evening

Wednesday

morning

Routine Tracker

afternoon

evening

Thursday

Friday

morning

morning

Routine Tracker

Routine Tracker

afternoon

afternoon

evening

evening

Saturday

morning

Routine Tracker

afternoon

What does rest look like for you today?

evening

Sunday

morning

Routine Tracker

afternoon

evening

Word Count Done

morning

Important This Week

- ⬡
- ⬡
- ⬡
- ⬡
- ⬡
- ⬡
- ⬡
- ⬡

WORD COUNT GOAL

Routine Tracker

☐ ☐ ☐ ☐ ☐

afternoon

evening

Tuesday	Wednesday
morning	morning
Routine Tracker	Routine Tracker
afternoon	afternoon
evening	evening

Thursday

Friday

morning

morning

Routine Tracker
□ □ □ □ □

Routine Tracker
□ □ □ □ □

afternoon

afternoon

evening

evening

Saturday

morning

Routine Tracker

afternoon

What does rest look like for you today?

evening

Sunday

morning

Routine Tracker

afternoon

evening

Word Count Done

MILK
HONEY
Books

Month of:

Monday

Important This Week

- ⬡
- ⬡
- ⬡
- ⬡
- ⬡
- ⬡
- ⬡
- ⬡

WORD COUNT GOAL

☐ morning

Routine Tracker

☐ ☐ ☐ ☐ ☐

afternoon

evening

morning

morning

Routine Tracker

☐ ☐ ☐ ☐ ☐

Routine Tracker

☐ ☐ ☐ ☐ ☐

afternoon

afternoon

evening

evening

MILK & HONEY Books

Thursday

Friday

morning

morning

Routine Tracker

☐ ☐ ☐ ☐ ☐

Routine Tracker

☐ ☐ ☐ ☐ ☐

afternoon

afternoon

evening

evening

Saturday

Sunday

morning

morning

Routine Tracker

Routine Tracker

afternoon

afternoon

What does rest look like for you today?

evening

evening

Word Count Done

MILK HONEY Books

Month of:

Monday

Important This Week

WORD
COUNT
GOAL

morning

Routine Tracker

afternoon

evening

Tuesday	Wednesday
morning	morning
Routine Tracker	Routine Tracker
afternoon	afternoon
evening	evening

Thursday

Friday

morning

morning

Routine Tracker

☐ ☐ ☐ ☐ ☐

Routine Tracker

☐ ☐ ☐ ☐ ☐

afternoon

afternoon

evening

evening

morning

morning

Routine Tracker

Routine Tracker

afternoon

afternoon

What does rest look like for you today?

evening

evening

Word Count Done

MILK HONEY Books

Month of:

Monday

morning

Important This Week

WORD
COUNT
GOAL

Routine Tracker

afternoon

evening

Tuesday

morning

Routine Tracker

afternoon

evening

Wednesday

morning

Routine Tracker

afternoon

evening

Thursday

Friday

morning

morning

Routine Tracker

Routine Tracker

afternoon

afternoon

evening

evening

morning

morning

Routine Tracker

Routine Tracker

afternoon

afternoon

What does rest look like for you today?

evening

evening

Word Count Done

MILK HONEY Books

Month of:

Monday

morning

Important This Week

Routine Tracker

afternoon

WORD
COUNT
GOAL

evening

Tuesday

Wednesday

morning

morning

Routine Tracker

Routine Tracker

afternoon

afternoon

evening

evening

MILK
HONEY
Books

Thursday

Friday

morning

morning

Routine Tracker

Routine Tracker

afternoon

afternoon

evening

evening

morning

morning

Routine Tracker

Routine Tracker

afternoon

afternoon

What does rest look like for you today?

evening

evening

Word Count Done

MILK
HONEY
Books

Notes

Lightning Source UK Ltd.
Milton Keynes UK
UKHW030102090221
378454UK00004B/224